Merry

Christmas

carol

Jesus

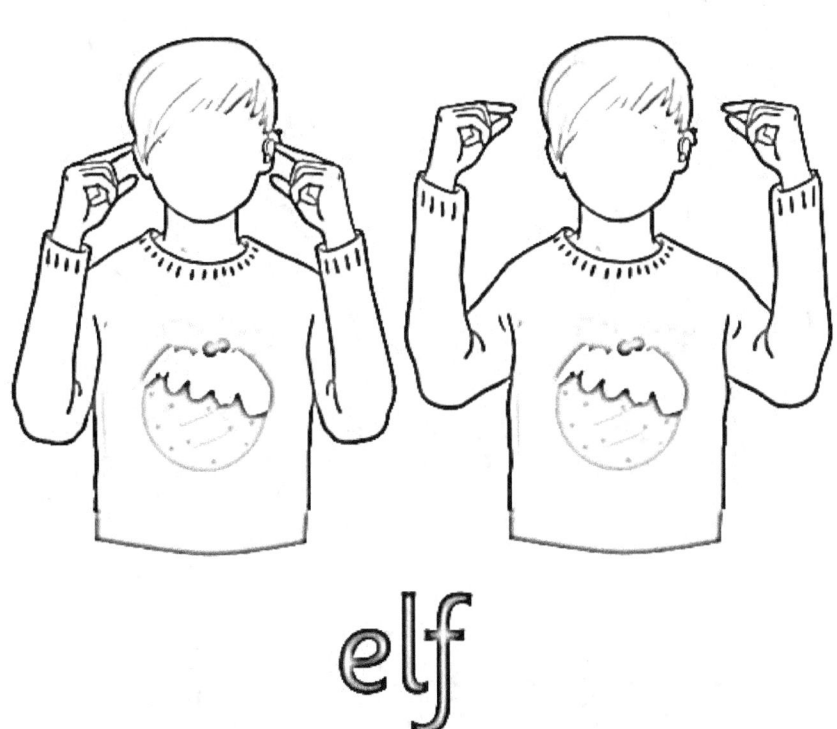

elf

mince pie

card

snow

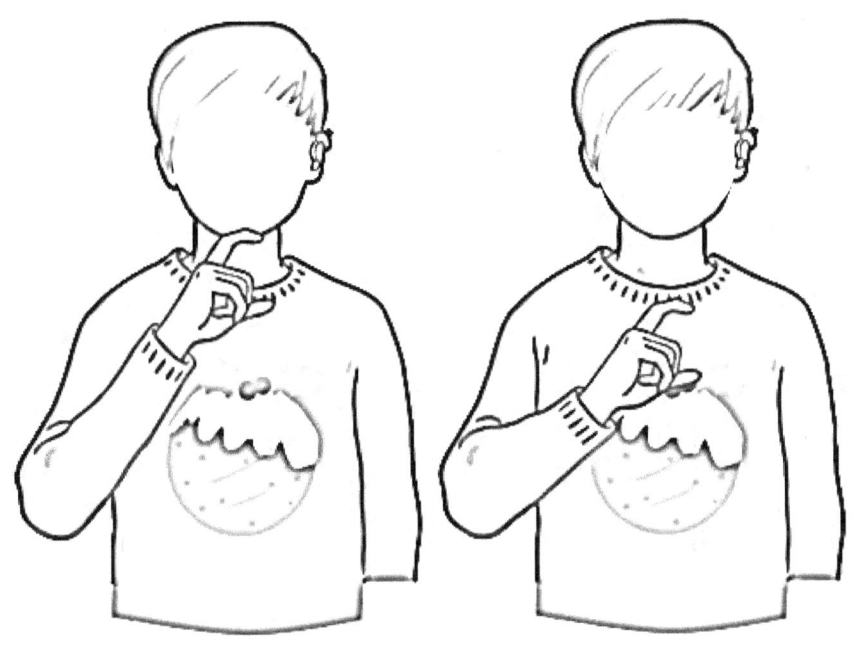

chocolate

Santa

reindeer

dinner

turkey

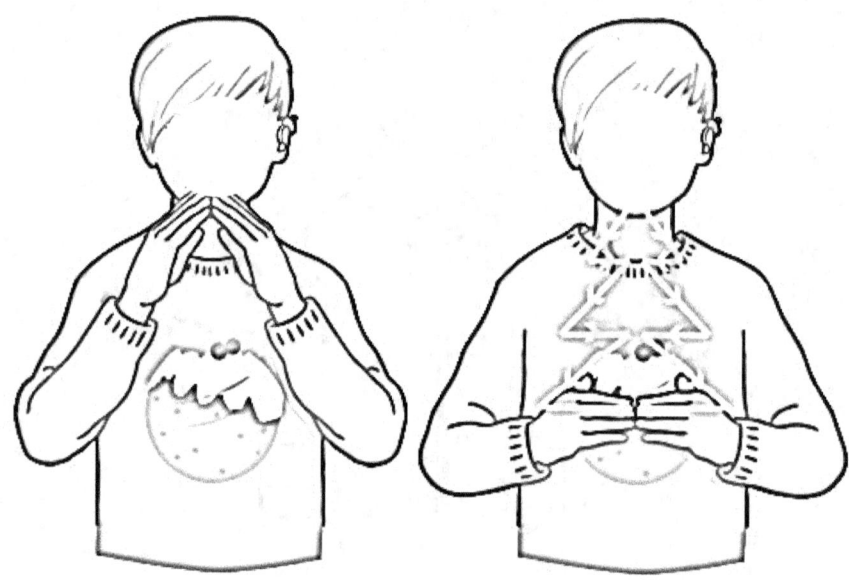

Christmas tree

merry

Christmas

cracker

angel

lights

pudding

church

story

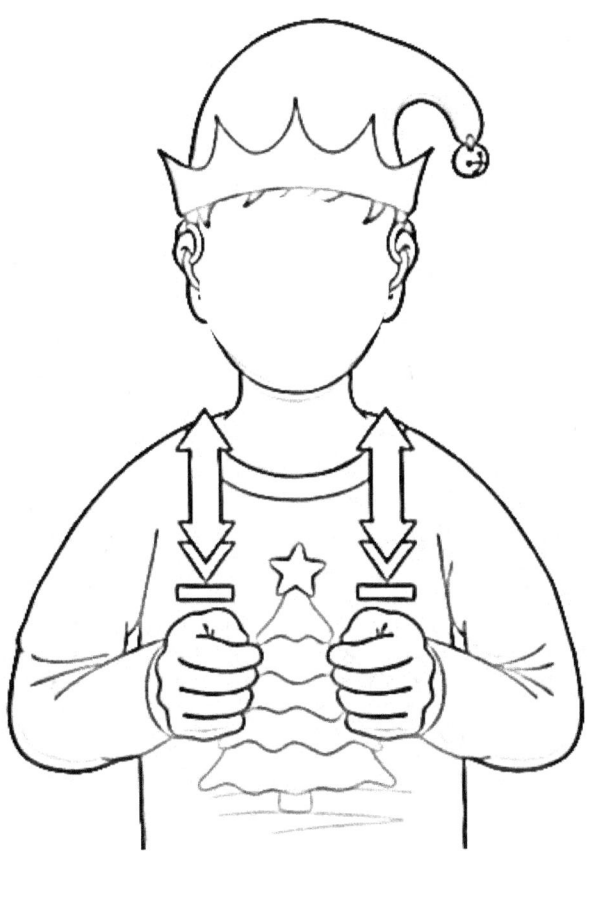

sleigh

snowman

toys

ice

snowball

paperchain

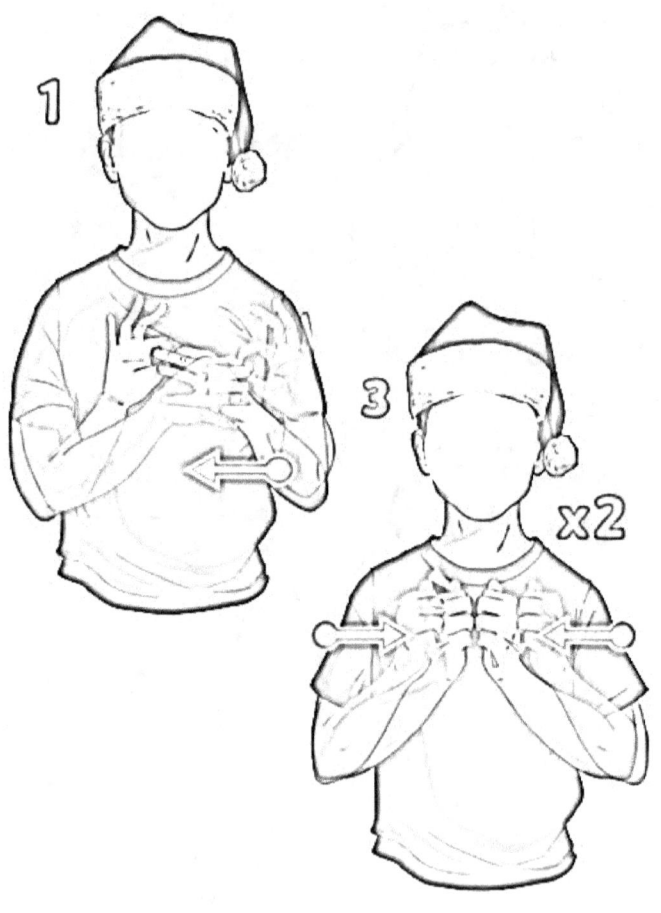

games

Christmas Eve

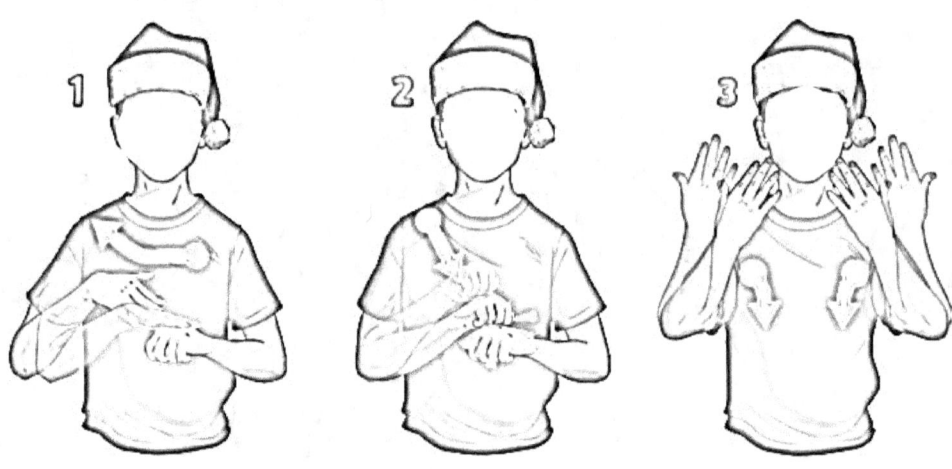

Christmas party

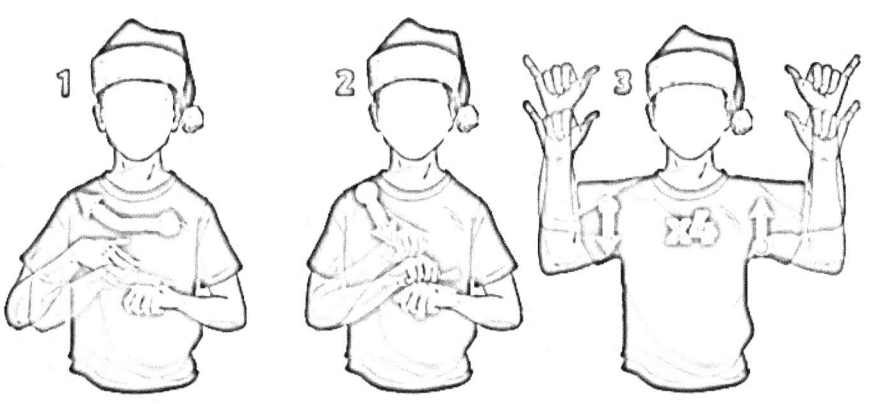

Christmas Day

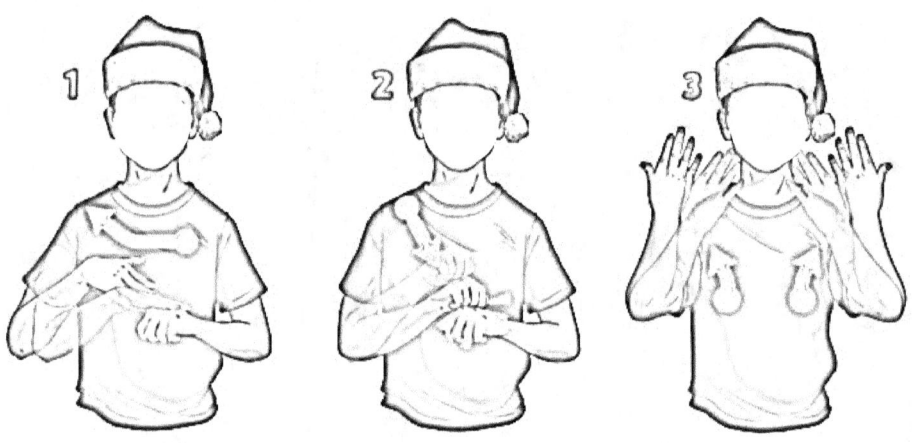

New Years Eve

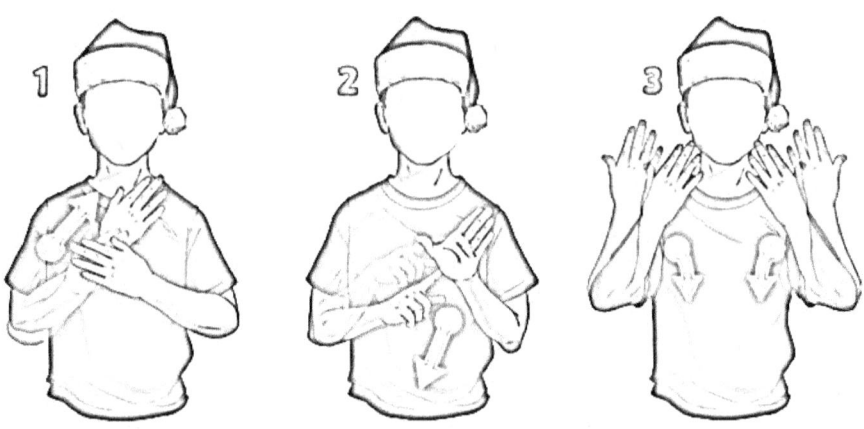

New Years Day

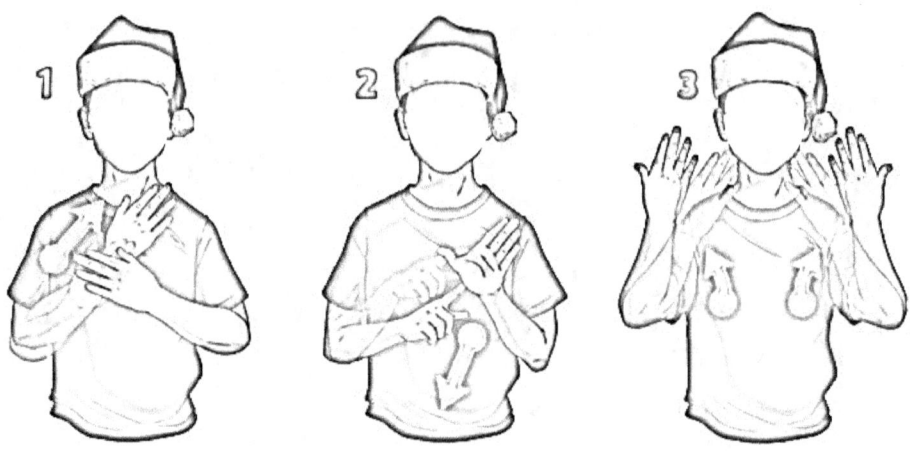

Thank you!

www.ingramcontent.com/pod-product-compliance
Lightning Source LLC
Chambersburg PA
CBHW072200060526
44654CB00046B/1366